The Goo
of Judgment

A Short Pastoral Theology

Chris MacBruithin

Rector of Castlerock and Dunboe, Diocese of Derry

GROVE BOOKS LIMITED

RIDLEY HALL RD CAMBRIDGE CB3 9HU

Contents

Acknowledgments

This book has developed from a thesis in biblical studies, which was supervised by Dr Katie Heffelfinger, an inspiring teacher and biblical scholar at the Church of Ireland Theological Institute, Dublin. Thanks are also due to the Grove Pastoral editorial group for encouraging me to write.

First Impression September 2021
ISSN 0144-171X
ISBN 978 1 78827 189 9

Introduction

1

> He's making a list
> He's checking it twice
> He's gonna find out who's naughty or nice
> Santa Claus is comin' to town
>
> *He sees you when you're sleeping*
> *He knows when you're awake*
> *He knows if you've been bad or good*
> *So be good for goodness sake!*[1]

You have likely heard this song coming up to Christmas. Personally, I find it rather creepy. For Christians, those pre-Christmas weeks are Advent, a season when we are especially mindful that Jesus 'will come again to judge the living and the dead.' But is that not like saying 'Santa Claus is comin' to town'? The threat of constant surveillance, of consequences for bad behaviour and the imminent arrival of a (mythical, to some) figure riding up there in the sky?

What do modern people think about divine judgment? For some Christians it is a theologically prominent and imminent reality to be dreaded. Images of standing alone before the throne, a record of one's life being publicly scrutinized, and fear of a fiery end, continue to trouble many believers during their lifetime. Are their crippling fear and shame necessary collateral damage for doctrinal faithfulness that judgment is coming? Where is the good news?

In mainstream churches, there is no liturgical getting away from judgment. Some in the congregation mentally cross their fingers for the line of the creed '[I believe] he will come again to judge the living and the dead.'[2] Advent prayers use language like 'cast away the works of darkness' and 'be ready' so that we 'may be found an acceptable people in thy sight.' At weddings, before vows are made, the officiant warns the couple that 'God, the judge of all, knows all the secrets of our hearts.' At funerals, the officiant talks about leaving the deceased 'in the keeping of God his/her creator, redeemer and judge.'

What if the pastor never elaborates on these terse statements, or says not to worry, 'It's just metaphorical'? People might wonder whether there might be something the preacher is not telling us. Should we be more worried about meeting Christ when we die? Failure to address ultimate questions might be as pastorally damaging as talking about it too much.

To the unchurched mind, the idea of judgment might seem risible, irrelevant or distinctly off-putting. We might think of bawling street preachers wearing sandwich boards. For millennials, 'judging' connotes mean and capricious panels on reality TV shows. Having made themselves vulnerable, participants are rejected the very moment they fail to impress. For many teenagers, judgment comes from cruel peers or editors of fat-shaming magazines. In their minds, why on Earth would it be good news that Jesus will come to be our judge?

Divine judgment is in fact good news for those in our pastoral care

I am convinced that divine judgment is in fact *good* news for those in our pastoral care. In the next chapter I will deal especially with people plagued by fear and shame at the thought of coming face to face with an angry God. I advocate deconstruction as a pastoral process of healing. This does not mean rejecting orthodox belief—I absolutely believe that 'He will come again to judge the living and the dead'—but instead, stripping away some of the unhelpful trappings that have accrued over the centuries.

The next stage is *re*construction. Some non-religious therapists assume that blanket religion is the problem and encourage clients to walk away from it wholesale. To reject a warped view of God as judge without some sort of restoration will not necessarily free an individual from the resulting feelings of fear, shame, victimhood or guilt. These are better worked through constructively towards an understanding of judgment that is critically informed, biblically faithful and pastorally responsible.

Consider Michelangelo's magnificent *The Last Judgment* in the Sistine Chapel. Earlier Christian art depicted an ethereal Jesus with a slight frame and a meek countenance. Michelangelo's fresco is very much a product of its cultural context, the Renaissance era. He paints a curly-haired Jesus with physiological realism, looking suspiciously like a Greek god. This Jesus scowls, raising his muscly right arm to cast aside the damned. Even his mother Mary looks terrified. As part of our cultural heritage, this iconic vista shapes our vision, but it was at first a shockingly new interpretation. Just because we have inherited it this way does not mean that it is accurate or original. The same goes for theology.

In the 1800s, Michelangelo's work needed restoration. Over the centuries, soot from altar candles had accumulated, as well as accretions like clothing painted in to protect the modesty of the damned. Likewise, our understanding of divine judgment may require restoration, a faithful return to the biblical original through the peeling away of some cultural and theological baggage.

Furthermore, Michelangelo's own judgment is coloured. He depicts his critic da Cesana among the hell-bound, adding donkey ears and, gruesomely, a serpent biting his genitals. He then paints himself into the scene as the flayed martyr St Bartholomew. Again, our theological views are coloured by personal experiences and biases. Sadly, in some religious settings, this doctrine is handled neither sensitively nor responsibly, but is weaponized as an instrument of hostility, self-justification and pastoral abuse.

How might belief in eschatological judgment actually resource the pastoral task? This book includes four encounters with victims of violence and crime, those in crisis or struggling with guilt, and the dying. Denise, Martin, Ray and Billy are composite characters based on my own ministerial experience. For them, and all in our care, judgment really is an integral part of the *good* news of Jesus Christ.

I have a personal stake in the topic of this book. 'Texts of terror' that keep little children awake at night are the subject of my ongoing research in biblical studies. In ministry, I come across people who struggle with shame and anxiety stemming from a religious upbringing that borders on the abusive, and for whom the idea of divine judgment still evokes terror. Finally, I was raised in a church like the first one I describe in chapter three.

For Reflection

- How do you feel about the credal statement, 'He will come again to judge the living and the dead'?
- What judgment have you experienced? Does it shape your view of God, for better or worse?
- Is presenting judgment as good news appropriate, or is it just an attempt to water down an unpopular belief?

2 Good News for the Fearful and Ashamed

Denise's Story

> No matter what I did, I felt guilty about something. I was terrified at the thought of standing in front of God, and everybody else finding out what I was really like, what I'd really done. I knew God loved me, but that nearly made it worse because I was such a bad person; maybe he loved me but he must be angry I wasn't a better person. It's hard; that childhood still comes back to haunt me.
>
> Denise

Until she went to university, Denise attended a fundamentalist, millenarian church. Behind the pulpit hung a six-foot long chart published by Clarence Larkin in 1918, depicting the end of the world.[3] Each event was assigned a time reference in relation to the precipitating event, the rapture. After seven years of tribulation and Christ's millennial reign, the Earth would burn up and all humanity be assembled before Christ's 'great white throne of judgment.' Sunday by Sunday, as a child and then a teenager, Denise stared at that image of Jesus and shuddered.

Larkin's chart and Denise's church are influenced by the dispensationalist theology of John Nelson Darby and C I Schofield. In their analysis, history is divided into seven dispensations. Neither the incarnation nor Jesus' Earthly ministry feature decisively in delineating these epochs. The 'dispensation of law' stretches from Moses to Christ's ascension. Then the current 'dispensation of grace' begins, with the church superseding Israel. The rapture will precipitate the seventh and final dispensation, including the final judgment.

This theological perspective has taken root especially in North America, where it is hugely influential in popular culture, such as Tim Lahaye and Jerry B Jenkins' famous *Left Behind* series. Dispensationalist belief influences politics too, from Middle East policy (if we spark a war, perhaps it will be Armageddon?) to environmental apathy (if the Earth will soon burn up, why legislate to protect the environment?).

However, our concern here is pastoral. The dispensationalist view of judgment is a source of anxiety for many devout Christians. As a child, Denise often lay awake plagued with fear and shame. Nightly, she would pray the sinner's prayer just in case it had not stuck last time. She could never tell anyone how she felt, of course. If she did, what would people think of her? Would she be exposed one day before the great white throne? Would others be there to eavesdrop on her account of her life? The thought terrified her.

After she left home, Denise found a new church. She has flourished in many ways, doing well at university and involved in her local church. However, she has never overcome that existential dread. She is still plagued by nagging doubts about her human worth and eternal destiny. At church, she experiences a certain cognitive dissonance. On one hand, the church is full of smiling faces and talk of Jesus' love and compassion. On the other hand, Denise is hyper-alert to mentions of divine judgment in Bible readings, prayers and hymns. She winces at the article in the creed that 'He will come again to judge the living and the dead.' What if her old church was right? Why are people here not more concerned about meeting God as their judge?

Existential Fear and Shame

Denise's experience is common among people recovering from an oppressively fundamentalist upbringing. Children in such contexts are vulnerable to psychosocial abuse, their behaviour regulated by fear, shame and punitive repercussions. In adulthood, having grown up with a primary understanding of God as an angry judge, Denise has internalized problems of low self-esteem. Other outcomes of iron-fisted end-times doctrine can include underdeveloped critical faculties, black-and-white thinking and an external locus of control that fosters passivity and pessimism.

Fear is easily co-opted by religious leaders as a strategy to manipulate

Fear and shame merit special attention. Fear is easily co-opted by religious leaders as a strategy to manipulate and control. Involvement with outsiders, the challenges of puberty and harbouring doubts or questions all become sources of anxiety. Feelings of impostor syndrome persist—fear of being exposed in this life or the next for what one really is or is not. Often, these fears are suppressed, again for fear that the response will be one of victim-shaming: 'If you're scared, then there must have been some reason why.'

Frequently, adults from such backgrounds have also internalized shame, an emotion that Brené Brown defines as the 'intensely painful feeling or experience of believing that we are flawed and therefore unworthy of love and belonging.'[4] Brown's research indicates that it is compounded by the silence that results from fear of being judged.

In Denise's case, the sustained burden of existential dread has taken its toll over her formative years, giving rise to clinical symptoms of depression and post-traumatic stress. When finally she confides in a pastor at her new church, hopefully this minister will understand that the pastor's role is sometimes to signpost to and work alongside qualified healthcare professionals and accredited therapists.

Some psychiatric disorders have a specifically religious component. Existential obsessive compulsive disorder involves disturbing and intrusive thoughts and behaviours about the big questions of life and death. It can manifest as scrupulosity, an anxiety-inducing fixation on one's religious and moral behaviour. For Denise, this takes the form of obsessively praying that she will get saved for fear that previous attempts were ineffective. This provides temporary relief from anxiety, but exacerbates the compulsive behaviour. Sufferers might present externally as paragons of Christian virtue; inwardly, they are crippled by fear and shame.

The Language of Judgment

Fundamentalism takes a flat prose view of language. Judge means judge. 'That's what the Bible says, and I just accept it.' Theological language does not work quite like this. When we call God Father, shepherd, rock or indeed judge, we are using analogies from human experience in order to speak of a God who transcends human language and comprehension. When we anthropomorphize God as shepherd, we know he does not hold a literal crook in his hand. Figurative language is the only way in which we humans can speak about God. It is also much more vivid and evocative than abstract conceptual statements.

Figurative language is the only way in which we humans can speak about God

Over time, language changes and new connotations develop around biblical metaphors. Many people feel uncomfortable today to refer to God as a warrior, for example. People in our pastoral care who have been abused might find it difficult to call God 'Father.' Victims of domestic abuse might bristle at the idea of the church as the bride of Christ. Sometimes the pastoral task involves rehabilitating images of God that have been tarnished but cannot easily be avoided. One of these is God as judge.

Theologian Jürgen Moltmann pinpoints a shift towards the literalizing of judgment on Constantine's adoption of Christianity as state religion, and the subsequent conflation of divine judgment with the Roman legal system, itself an instrument of fear and control.[5] People who have grown up in fundamentalist communities often conflate God with ideas they associate with judge, whether or not these are appropriate: absolute authority to silence and sentence, caprice, anger, establishment, remote. It might be popular culture or paternalistic dominance that forms such understanding.

Furthermore, in dispensationalist discourse, 'judge' becomes a controlling analogy over and above others like father and shepherd. It becomes necessary then to strip away the wig and gown of the courthouse judge, the scathing evaluation of the reality TV panel, and the piercing criticism of bullies on SnapChat. This deliteralizing is part of a critical process called deconstruction.

Deconstruction and Reconstruction

Deconstruction involves taking apart elements of one's belief system for critical re-examination. The aim is reconstruction of that faith system, with new understanding of complexity and nuance. Typically, this process is undergone by ministerial students in Bible colleges and seminaries, grappling with difficult questions and considering alternative viewpoints. They usually receive special support. It can be a frightening and disorienting experience to question long-held beliefs, often entailing a sense of loss. There is fear of a slippery slope: if this one thing is 'just metaphorical,' what is to say the rest is still true? The ideal outcome is for graduates to emerge with a deepened, more robust faith.

It can be helpful or even necessary for someone troubled by existential fear or shame to undergo a similar process, guided by a sensitive pastor. For people emerging from fundamentalist backgrounds who have never been allowed to transition from stage to stage in their faith, there can be a crash akin to a computer whose updates have been ignored too long. Sadly, many victims of heavy pastoring and spiritual abuse see no alternative other than to reject the Christian faith wholesale and walk away. Others stay, secretly plagued by fear and shame for the duration of their lives. They may suppress their experience, appearing ultra-religious to others, with the undealt-with fear and shame manifesting as anger or destructive behaviours.

How then can the pastor accompany and support someone whose faith and well-being are impaired by fear and shame? How can we responsibly manage the deconstruction process in such an encounter, so as not to leave the person before us in confusion, despair or tempted to give up completely? Rational persuasion might help, but there is the risk of descending into arguments about the nature of theological language and trading Bible verses. And the emotional feedback loops of fear and shame are rooted in a more basal part of the brain than the stuff of grey matter.

Meeting Jesus in the Gospels

Someone terrified by the idea of facing Christ on judgment day will benefit from encountering him in advance. Christians believe that God has made himself known in the person of Jesus Christ, revealed to us in Scripture. Hopefully, Scripture is integral to all our pastoral work, whether in the public form of preaching and teaching, to families at times of special need such as illness and bereavement, or in encounters with individuals like Denise who seek our help. It is especially in the pages of the gospels that we see who this man is who will be our judge; the sort of things he says; how he treats people.

I believe that Denise's understanding of divine judgment is dangerously distorted, with scant regard for the person and nature of Jesus. The doctrine that formed her view consigns the earthly ministry of Jesus, including his ethical teaching and compassionate responses to 'sheep without a shepherd,' to a past, pre-grace dispensation. Stories of healing, radical forgiveness and inclusion are treated as mere incidentals in a long preface to the passion accounts, where we see the full, bloody measure of divine wrath. The result is a skewed and deficient understanding of God, with devastating pastoral ramifications. Denise can remember every detail of Larkin's 'Seventh Dispensation' chart, but has engaged shockingly little with the Jesus of the gospels.

I find it telling that in my own Church of Ireland's (Anglican) Healing Service, a reading from one of Matthew, Mark, Luke or John is prescribed. The underlying assumption seems to be that healing takes place in an encounter with Jesus, and while all Scripture points forward and back to him, it is in the four gospels that we see him most clearly. As a form of healing, deliverance from fear and shame requires Jesus' presence. What more would a pastor want than this, to see God's beloved children healed and liberated in an encounter with the Lord?

A Guided Meditation

Ignatian spirituality provides a particularly imaginative way of experiencing Jesus in the gospels. It helps us see and hear, ask questions and put ourselves in the place of the disciples, crowds and others involved. It is rooted in prayer. A pastoral encounter with Denise, using Ignatian-style Bible reading, might go something like this:

> Denise, my role today is to help you encounter the Lord Jesus.
>
> First, let's sit quietly. As we sit, become aware of your thoughts and feelings. Why are you here? What is on your heart? *(Pause. Denise may speak at this point, or may remain silent.)*

Now, become aware that you are in Christ's presence. He is here with us. He knows you and he loves you. *(Silence)*

I'm going to read Mark 8.22–25.

They came to Bethsaida. Some people brought a blind man to him and begged him to touch him. He took the blind man by the hand and led him out of the village; and when he had put saliva on his eyes and laid his hands on him, he asked him, 'Can you see anything?' And the man looked up and said, 'I can see people, but they look like trees, walking.' Then Jesus laid his hands on his eyes again; and he looked intently and his sight was restored, and he saw everything clearly. (NRSV)

Who is in the scene? Where is it? Imagine the sights, sounds, smells, time of day. What is happening, and why?

Why did the people think to bring the blind man to Jesus? Why do they want Jesus to touch him (rather than speak to him, or have him touch Jesus' cloak)?

Jesus takes the man by the hand and leads him out of the village. Why?

Jesus spits on the man's eyes and asks, 'Can you see anything?' What is his vision like at this point?

The man needs a second touch before his vision becomes clear. What does this mean to you?

Jesus looked intently on the man he was healing, and his sight was restored. Imagine what that man saw. The first face he has seen in years, perhaps ever. What does Jesus' face look like?

At this point, it would be useful to check with Denise how she sees Jesus' face. Hopefully, the context of the story and the guiding of the Spirit of Christ have led her to a loving, compassionate, gentle mental image.

Denise, this is the same Lord Jesus who is with you now. That same face is gazing intently on you. We ask him now to restore your sight so you can see him clearly.

Now talk to him freely. What do you want to say to him?

End in prayer, concluding with the words: 'Lord Jesus, you are the same yesterday, today and forever. Amen.'

For Reflection

- If you were to paint a picture of Christ at the final judgment, what would his face look like?

- In your own life, has your understanding of an aspect of Christian belief changed or developed? How did that happen?
- What other Bible passage(s) could you use with Denise?

Good News for Victims

3

> Remember, O Lord, against the Edomites, the day of Jerusalem's fall,
> how they said, 'Tear it down! Tear it down! Down to its foundations!'
> O daughter Babylon, you devastator!
>
> Happy shall they be who pay you back what you have done to us!
> Happy shall they be who take your little ones
> and dash them against the rock!
>
> Ps 137.7–9
>
> If I ever find the man who did this to my little girl,
> I swear to God, I'll kill him.
>
> Martin

Marie could have been Catholic or Protestant, a police officer or a civilian; it does not matter. She was killed by terrorists during the 'Troubles' in Northern Ireland. For her father Martin, justice was never done. Since her shooting in the 1980s, no one has been convicted. At a grassroots level, people know who was involved. But the peace process has, in his view, required that too much be brushed under the carpet. Peace and reconciliation are all well and good, thinks Martin, but they have come at the cost of justice.

He attends church weekly, partly because he feels close to Marie there, but he often bristles at the words he hears: God loves and accepts everybody, just ask and God will forgive. If the men who killed Marie escaped justice in this life, it sounds like God will be a soft touch in the next.

'Remember, O Lord'

Few passages have the capacity to shock with raw honesty like Psalm 137 above. This post-traumatic lament is not in fact sung *in* Babylon where the deportees are exiled. That was 'there' (v 1). God's people have returned to their devastated homeland some 40 years later. Yet the intervening decades have not brought healing. The memory is as painful as ever. The psalm culminates in an imprecation which, in public worship, our Western sensibilities urge us to omit. Commentators argue that the violent image is figurative or hyperbolic. But even if we deliteralize the incitement to infanticide, the psalmist still hopes his enemies are obliterated from the face of the Earth.

The psalmist has not forgotten Babylon's attack on Jerusalem, cheered on by Judah's Edomite cousins. As both witness and prosecution, he describes the atrocity in terms of a savage rape. In Hebrew, Jerusalem is 'she,' not 'it.' Edom's exclamation, 'Tear her down' can be rendered 'Strip her' or 'Lay her bare.' 'Foundations' are synonymous with buttocks or thighs. Piecing these details together yields a gut-wrenching image of rape that could be rendered 'Pull her down! Strip her bare!' God's people have been utterly violated, and the psalmist vows never to forget.

Neither can we today forget, because this cry for justice has become part of our canon of Scripture. We might join in, 'Remember, O Lord, against' Nazis who fled to Chile and grew old, child abusers who die peacefully in their sleep, police officers who brutalize Black citizens and indeed the paramilitaries who shot Martin's daughter Marie.

Like the captives in Babylon, Martin often sits, weeps and vows never to forget what happened. Marie's life mattered, and it was taken from her. An awful injustice was done and has never been put right. But as cathartic as the weeping and recounting are, is remembering enough? Can Martin, or indeed Marie, ever see justice done? When we urge God to 'Remember, O Lord, against' the wicked, do we do so because we fear God has forgotten, does not care, or is so merciful and loving that he is soft on crime? Martin confesses, 'I don't want the comfort of a God who doesn't do anything to change it.'

The Biblical Judge

Imagine you are an Israelite widow or orphan. One day, a property developer decides to extend his portfolio and he demolishes your humble dwelling to make way. If you had a husband or father (this is a patriarchal society), he might have stood up to oppose this wicked man. However, you know that this developer has contravened God's law, so you cannot wait for the one person to come to town who can help you: the *shophet*, the judge.

Moses is the Bible's first *shophet*. It is necessary to maintain justice and peace in the Hebrew community as they travel across Sinai. In Exod 18.13–27, Moses spends a whole day arbitrating complaints. His father-in-law observes him in this demanding role and contends that his practice is 'not good.' There are too many interpersonal disputes for one individual to adjudicate. Moses heeds Jethro's advice. He identifies and appoints capable, God-fearing and honest people to the office of judge, reserving for himself the most complex cases.

After the Israelites settle the land, judges are appointed in each city (Deut 16.18–17.13; 19.15–21). They sit at the city gate, accessible to anyone, rich or poor. This legal updating for life in the promised land suggests there has been experience of corruption. It has become needful to specify the role of the judge as rendering just decisions on the basis of thorough inquiry and interpreting laws in complex cases. The deuteronomist forbids corrupt practices like nepotism and bribery. Witnesses are now required to give evidence, and there are severe penalties for perjury. A higher court in Jerusalem handles the most complex cases, and its decision is binding. These provisions and prohibitions evidence that the judiciary, like any human institution, even one divinely appointed, is imperfect.

By the time of the classical prophets, a stinging critique of the judiciary is warranted (Amos 5.10–15; Isa 10.1–4). At the city gate, supposedly the place where justice is done and seen to be done, judges are casting aside the poor, who have no grain to offer as a bribe, and passing unfair and oppressive laws that deprive widows and orphans of their rights. God's response will be to judge the judges. The prophets foretell the Assyrian and Babylonian invasions and a decisive reckoning, the coming 'Day of YHWH.'

In the aftermath of the Babylonian crisis lamented in Psalm 137, God's people enter into a period of intense theological reflection. Like contemporary victims of violent crimes, they ask, 'Why did God let this happen? Is it divine judgment? Is God unable to help us, or unwilling?'

The outcome of this period of theological and pastoral reflection in Babylon is both realistic and hopeful. It acknowledges evil and suffering, and the absence of justice in the present. It also looks forward to a decisive day when God will somehow make things right. This is not amnesia of what happened, but the vindication of the victim. When an authoritative judge rules against the oppressor, the ground somehow moves. Too many innocent victims never get to see justice done in their lifetime, but *they will see justice done*. Upon mature reflection, post-exilic Jews cling to this hope: since God is both good and sovereign, then if justice has not been done, it is not the end.

Innocent victims will see justice done

Victim Support

How do we minister to those denied justice in this life? UK charity Victim Support accompanies those affected from crime to court and beyond.[6] Their 'journey' approach illumines the pastoral task even as broken humanity awaits the decisive judgment in heaven. The pastor's job is to accompany and support the victim along this journey, pointing out how God is involved throughout, and to aid the victim's transition from one stage to the next.

The journey outlined by Victim Support begins as soon as the offence is committed. Of course, God's jurisdiction extends beyond what legally constitutes a crime, and the same pastoral support can therefore be extended to victims of non-criminal injustices like adultery. The pastor at this stage should listen attentively and take the person seriously, as would the police (one hopes). Counselling techniques come to the fore here. It is important to move forward through the paraphrasing and head-nodding of active listening, towards the victim naming the offence and concluding that they are not to blame. Martin above needs to be empowered to say, 'My daughter was murdered by terrorists. That was wrong and she deserves justice.'

Martin's journey is hampered by the fact that no one has been—nor is likely to be—prosecuted for his daughter's killing. The reality is that prosecution for certain crimes may not be deemed to be in the public interest. Police may have insufficient resources to investigate, there may be insufficient evidence to bring a case to court, and trials collapse due to legal technicalities and loopholes. Victims often feel let down, despondent, angry or incredulous at the lack of justice.

Christians believe that justice will be done even in such circumstances, because God will ensure it, at an ultimate reckoning of history in the eschaton. Rushing the journey towards acceptance of this point, as if it should make everything instantly bearable, would be hugely counterproductive. In *Praying the Psalms,* Walter Brueggemann identifies stages of orientation, disorientation and reorientation.[7] The author of Psalm 137 remembers a time when life seemed fair. The savage attack on Jerusalem and deportation of her population disoriented the psalmist. Life suddenly seems chaotic, blighted with unwarranted and random suffering. Psalm 137 is written for this stage of anger, confusion and pain. The sensitive pastor knows when and how to gently reorient the individual to eschatological hope, without denying the time needed to receive the impact and for necessary catharsis.

Rushing the journey towards acceptance would be hugely counterproductive

When brought to court, Victim Support volunteers accompany victims of crime. They ensure clients know what will happen and that they are heard and understood. They ensure that victims' needs are met, including the opportunity to state publicly how the crime has affected them. In an overstretched, imperfect legal system, this may require advocacy as well as emotional support, even as we await God's ultimate, salvific judgment in heaven.

Belief in a final judgment at the end of history undergirds any pastoral response to a victim of crime or someone let down by the justice system. The fact is that no victim's journey is over while the injustice they have suffered remains unresolved. In the pastoral journey, the anguish of Psalm 137 must be given voice, but it is not the terminal point. For people like Martin, reorientation towards trust in God's ultimate right-making is crucial to not becoming stuck in his imprecation, nor being defined by victimhood.

For Reflection

- Who in your pastoral context might find the hope that God's justice extends beyond death especially important?
- Where does forgiveness fit in?

4

Good News in a Crisis

Judgment as Crisis

In the 1960s, US scientists realized that no new giant sequoia trees were growing, and the reason was the overly successful control of wildfires. They discovered that wildfires are a necessary part of nature. They create warm updraughts, drying cones and allowing seeds to fall. Fire clears debris, returning valuable nutrients to the soil and making space for germinating seeds. Today, Californian authorities sometimes start controlled fires as part of the lifecycle of local flora. Forest fires promote new life.

Sometimes, the same can be said of crises. It is hard to understand how they could possibly be God's design. But if they cause us to rethink our lives and our Christian faith, like forest fires, they might clear the way for new beginnings.

In ministry to people in crisis, we often hear the most difficult of questions: 'Is this God's judgment?' In English, crisis and judgment sound like two very different things. In fact, crisis derives from the New Testament Greek word *krisis*, which means judgment. The problem is that in most crises the innocent suffer alongside the guilty. Consider the case of Ray.

In most crises the innocent suffer alongside the guilty

Ray has lost his job after a series of redundancies at his company. He does not know how he will provide for his family and meet his financial commitments beyond a few months. It is not only a matter of salary. His confidence has been shattered. How could this happen after a decade of loyalty and hard work? Now with too much time on his hands, he gets to wondering whether the job was redundant, or *he* was. Will he get another job at his age? Are his skills, acquired over a lifetime, no longer of value? Ray is in an existential as well as a financial crisis.

This personal crisis is not the result of any wrongdoing on his part. He did not mismanage company finances. His job loss is not divine punishment. His situation constitutes judgment in quite a different way: a present time of acute difficulty, a critical moment in which Ray will see what he is really made of.

One day, we will all give account of our time on Earth, and for Ray that will include not only this redundancy but what he makes of the situation. Cardinal Basil Hume explains post-mortem judgment like this: 'Judgment is whispering into the ear of a merciful and compassionate God the story of my life which I have never been able to tell.'[8]

How will Ray narrate his current situation on that day? Looking back, will it be an important episode, perhaps even a decisive or ultimate one? Will he tell his story with tears, a clenched fist, or a resigned shrug? Or will he follow on with an overcoming, a subsequent twist in the story arc?

Ray will do well to do what God's people have done throughout Scripture—to reframe the narrative of his life. If there is a judgment in the here and now, it constitutes a critical moment of self understanding, drawing on his inner resources and possibly taking a definitive new step in the unfolding of his life. If life is essentially chaotic and unjust, then Ray is in a dead-end situation. If he believes in God, and can imagine himself giving an account of what he did with his life, then he might more easily frame this personal crisis as part of a wider plot of overcoming and renewal.

Life as Narrative

Ray has never heard of French philosopher Paul Ricoeur. However, his pastor might find resources in Ricoeur's theory that our lives are narratively configured.[9] We experience novels and movies as meaningful because they are narratives about people. When we leave the cinema, we discuss the film, not to rehearse the order of events mentally, but to make human sense of it. What has it to say about the human condition? How satisfying was the ending? We are thus all critics in this way (that is, judges), evaluating the success or otherwise of human stories.

We do not make sense of our lives as chronicles, one event after another

We do not make sense of our lives as chronicles, one event after another. We select some episodes as meaningful and choose to de-emphasize others because they do not say anything significant about who we are and what it means that we exist in the world. The episodes to which we attach special significance, we configure as part of our personal narrative. Once a narrative identity is formed, it can become quite resistant to change. We are less likely to integrate new experiences of the world into our lives if they threaten the stability of our self-understanding. It sometimes takes a crisis to trigger change or growth.

Episodes are configured narratively by a process of 'emplotment.' When another person does something to us, or we do something to them, we instinctively infer cause and effect, motives and evaluations. Over time, in the story we construct, we might be the brave protagonist, the dependable supporting character, the lovable rogue or the victim. When we integrate only those life experiences that bolster our perceived self-identity, and suppress those that challenge the story we tell about ourselves, we can become brittle and resistant to change.

The redundancy has jolted Ray out of the homeostasis of his self-understanding. His challenge now is to integrate his job loss and associated loss of sense of self within the wider life story that he will whisper into God's ear at his life's end. In order to help Ray emplot this story, his pastor will benefit from some knowledge of scriptural examples of narrative reframing following a crisis, as well as some techniques used in spiritual direction.

A New Testament Crisis Narrative

In chapter three, we considered the Babylonian invasion and exile, a formative chapter in Jewish self-understanding. With no temple, faith had to become more word-centred and interior. Scripture was written down and consolidated and a bigger, international understanding of God's saving purposes developed. Not only did Judaism survive, but the exiles responded with a more mature vision of God's purposes and their role in the world.

N T Wright challenges many of our assumptions about judgment in his treatment of the imminent crisis of divine judgment in the synoptic tradition.[10] A traditional reading of Jesus' predictions in Mark 13 is that these refer to a final judgment at the end of history. Wright urges a historical reading, based on his masterful reconstruction of the worldview and experience of second temple Judaism.

The fall of the second temple is a national crisis waiting to happen

As Wright configures the gospel narrative, the fall of the second temple in 70 AD is a national crisis waiting to happen. Jesus sees it as an inevitable outcome of religious intransigence and national chauvinism. Jesus' predictions come true, of course. Those impressive temple stones are brought crashing down in Rome's violent response to the Jewish uprising. The cosmic imagery of heavenly bodies falling from the heavens and the celestial bodies going dark convey metaphorically the depth of the political and religious crisis.

Even if Jesus' disciples are forewarned, it is an awful crisis. They know to flee to the hills for safety. Jesus tells them to pray that this displacement will not take place in winter. It will be especially hard for pregnant and nursing mothers. Those who do not heed the warning to flee will be violently killed or else led away as captives to Rome. Either before or after the destruction of the city (or both), Jesus' disciples will be the victims of tremendous persecution, including by their own families.

This suffering is not to be minimized by platitudes. However, because of their displacement, Jesus' disciples are scattered across the region, throughout Judea, into Samaria and beyond. In their crisis, these people show determination and strength, and bring the good news of Jesus all around the known world. Where they could have despaired and given up hope, they in fact respond to this critical moment by initiating a whole new chapter in salvation history. Judaism is reconfigured as a religion of the book. Christianity becomes an international, cross-cultural and dynamic movement.

In this New Testament narrative, God's people emerge from a crisis with a renewed faith and self-understanding. So how can this help Ray?

Spiritual Direction

Spiritual directors listen attentively to their directees over a period of time, helping them to speak openly and honestly about their ongoing experience of God in their lives. Difficult experiences are probed, with attention given to discerning God at work and to integrating change and challenge into our lives and identities. Gaining insight is important, but the 'direction' in spiritual direction is crucial. This is about where the story of our lives might go from here, transformed and renewed. Ray will not get his old job back, and the experience of redundancy cannot be erased from his life. The question is, what will he do next?

Looking at the narrative setting of Ray's job loss, a spiritual director or pastor might be interested when Ray discloses that he had been unsatisfied in his job for some time, and considered quitting on two occasions. People have told him over the years that he should consider going self-employed—he certainly has the contacts. On the other hand, his own sector is not thriving as it once was. There are opportunities for retraining.

Ray has been working long hours with no overtime paid. When his children were small, he regularly arrived home from work after their bedtime, and he often missed school plays and football matches. His wife has long accused him of giving his all at work and leaving her and the children with the dregs at the weekend. He got out of the habit of church attendance several years ago when he decided that Sunday mornings were best used to reduce his sleep deficit.

One question often posed by a spiritual director is 'Where is the gift in this situation?' For all the talk of opportunity and *kairos* moments, 'gift' is theologically a better word. It conveys not the individual's initiative but God's grace already at work. To a people experiencing loss, distress and bewilderment following the crisis of the Babylonian invasion, God says through the prophet Jeremiah, 'The people who survive the sword will find grace in the wilderness' (Jer 31.2). When we say that judgment is divine, this actually means that

God is at work in our crises, not throwing them down at us like thunderbolts. Crises can present the gift of God at work in our lives in a particular, if not easy, way. Spiritual direction helps to identify where exactly that gift lies.

The temptation will be to offer chipper platitudes about silver linings. But we can go a step further in directing Ray to integrate this experience into the next part of his life. We can help him to begin imagining and rehearsing the story that he would choose to whisper into God's ear—knowing that we will meet God and undergo a judgment is a gift. When we know this in advance, we can prepare for it. We know there is ultimate value to our lives and what we do with them.

One imaginative approach is the Ignatian spiritual exercise of writing one's own obituary. What story will we finally whisper into God's ear? This is an exercise to be completed prayerfully upon much reflection, hopefully under the care of a pastor who is skilled at helping people to integrate crisis situations into a wider whole, to tell their stories and to an extent write them. They know when to support people as they receive the impact of a diagnosis, bereavement or other life crisis, and crucially to recognize the critical moment in which to encourage people to begin writing the next chapter. Both the process and end product of writing are useful for considering how our lives are impacted by crises.

In a satisfying narrative, the protagonist must undergo some sort of ordeal. Otherwise there is not much of a story! In the narrative arc, this is not just one more event after another but the crisis, which initiates the protagonist's quest and leads to a do-or-die moment. Also, in any good novel, the protagonist will emerge transformed, perhaps more self-confident or suitably humbled, having dealt with a past failure or overcome a longstanding fear. An easy victory or *deus ex machina* plot resolution is terribly unsatisfying for the reader. Just as coming through a crisis is essential to a good novel, so too our response to personal crises in our own lives are decisive for how satisfying a life we narrate for ourselves. We cannot control the crisis, but we can shape our response to it.

Ray Tells His Story

On judgment day, Ray could whisper this story into God's ear:

> I worked my guts out for that company. I sacrificed my family, my health. And then I got a letter saying thank you for your 14 years of service but there's no job for you here any more. That was it. Out of my hands. And at my age, younger people were coming in with all these new skills—who was going to take me on? I know, I should have made the time to go to church. Maybe then you'd have given me my

> job back? I suppose I should be thankful that at least I saw more of the grandchildren than I ever did my own growing up.

It is not a great story. Ray uses his redundancy as an excuse for not doing more with his life. This version of events betrays an external locus of control. Ray considers himself the victim of circumstances, unfairly treated in light of all he gave. There is no sign of recovery or new life, merely a begrudging acknowledgment of a silver lining. What might God's evaluation be of this story? How will God judge Ray's response to the gift he had?

On the other hand, if Ray can reframe his redundancy experience as a critical moment, the judgment day conversation might go more like this:

> In hindsight, losing that job was the making of me. It was only when I stopped that I realized what I'd been missing. Imagine if I'd kept going at break-neck pace until I had a heart attack! I'd lost track of what was important.
>
> I'd always wanted to be a teacher, but I thought I'd missed the boat, never brave enough to bite the bullet, resign and miss out a year's salary and retrain. Redundancy forced my hand, and I did it. Ten years in the classroom, at that stage in my life! And then in retirement to meet all those young people who stopped me and said, 'Mr Maguire, you taught me business studies at school,' and then they'd tell me what they did after school and how I'd inspired them.

For Reflection

- When have you or someone you know wondered 'Is this God's judgment?'
- Can you see a time in your life when a personal crisis instigated positive transformation?

5 Good News at the Eleventh Hour

Our final pastoral task is end-of-life care for Billy. He has recently been told by the oncologist that the cancer has spread. It is now a matter of palliative care.

Billy is aware like never before of his own mortality. If doctors are right, he will stand before his creator, redeemer and judge within months. From the question he poses, it is clear to the hospital chaplain what is on Billy's mind:

> Do you think God is a vengeful God?

In honesty, it has sometimes been difficult to minister to Billy over the course of his illness. Decades of civil conflict in Northern Ireland have left him bitter and intransigent. A staunch Protestant loyalist, he frequently rails against his 'enemies' on 'the other side,' meaning Roman Catholics. He complains about the foreign doctors, and claims his medical treatment has suffered because immigrants are 'bleeding the system dry.' At 76, housebound and with just months to live, the chaplain wonders deep down what she can do. But then Billy's question surfaces. Why is he concerned to know whether in death the God he has claimed as Ulster Protestants' tribal deity will be vengeful?

Until just now, Billy did not seem remorseful about much in his life. But now, a terminal diagnosis has evoked fear of what God might make of it. If he is honest with himself, Billy knows he is prone to comparing the worst in others with an idealized version of himself. He was not exactly at home sipping cocoa every night while proscribed organizations were swapping information and hatching plans.

Anti-heroes and Villains

Let us return to life as narrative. Billy is afraid to meet God, not so much due to a distorted view like Denise's in chapter two, but because he harbours guilty secrets. He realizes that when he whispers the story he has constructed of his life—the story he has told others and himself over the years—into God's merciful ear, God will detect elements of self-deception and hypocrisy.

A most satisfying plot development in a narrative, one that speaks deeply to the human condition, is the redemption of the anti-hero or villain. From the beginning, we know Harry Potter will rise to the challenge.[11] It is not so with Severus Snape, Hogwarts' acerbic potions master with an interest in the dark arts. As readers, we long for him to get his come-uppance, to be exposed for the man he is and his mean treatment of Harry in particular. However, Rowling does what only great storytellers can do when she redeems her seemingly unlovable villain. If the hospital chaplain is as good a pastor as Rowling is a writer, she will know that her job is not done while Billy is breathing.

Rowling gradually discloses Snape's backstory. Potter's father bullied him as a child, and he was heartbroken by unrequited love for Potter's mother. We come to realize that Snape's coldness, cynicism and severity have their roots in his pain, rejection and shame. Secondly, even when he collaborates with Voldemort's forces of evil, there is always the option of redemption. Snape could choose to go in either direction, but redeems himself in an eleventh-hour decision for good.

If Severus Snape is redeemable, then surely Jesus Christ who has lived our humanity and been tempted as we are, yet without sin, will show understanding in his judgment of Billy's life. It is not about making excuses, but understanding another human life in its complexity and ambiguity. As a teenager growing up in rural 1950s Northern Ireland, Billy only heard what his parents and neighbours told him. He heard when Catholic militia beat up loyalist comrades, but not about loyalists burning Catholic neighbours out of their homes. Billy grew up with a siege mentality. He believed that Ulster was a land given to Protestant people, just like the promised land of the Israelites in the Bible. Catholics were like Canaanites: stubborn, pagan and to be routed.

Realistically, Billy does not possess the time or opportunity to live out the consequences of a fundamental narrative transformation. He will not become a hero or moral example. Nonetheless, by God's grace, redemption is always available. Neither is this a case of Billy earning salvation by works. The anti-hero Zacchaeus' redemption includes the fourfold repayment of any amount he may have overcharged, but when Jesus gives a reason why 'Today salvation has come to this house,' the basis is God's determination to seek out and find lost sinners (Luke 19.1–10). His grace is always prevenient to our response.

Confession as Reconciliation

Returning to Basil Hume's understanding of post-mortem judgment, Billy will soon whisper his life story to God. This is causing him distress in his palliative state, because he realizes that his defence mechanisms of suppressing and justifying his failures will be shown up before God our judge. Hume continues with specific reference to contrition:

> Many of us have a story, or part of one at any rate, about which we have never been able to speak to anyone. Fear of being misunderstood.

Inability to understand ourselves. Ignorance of the darker side of our hidden lives, or just shame, make it very difficult for many people. The true story of our life is not told, or only half of it is. What a relief it will be to be able to whisper freely and fully into that merciful and compassionate ear. After all, that is what he has always wanted. He receives us, his prodigal children, now contrite and humble, with an embrace.[12]

Whether or not we consider it a sacrament of the church, confession is a gift. In gathered worship, it often takes the form of a general confession within preparation for worship as we approach a holy God. Now, as Billy prepares to meet God face to face, he might benefit from individual confession. As the maxim goes, 'All may; none must; some should.' I would suggest that Billy should!

We sometimes view confession as a procedure of balancing accounts. In the Roman Catholic Church, confession has been renamed the sacrament of reconciliation. Reconciliation is a better word because it is about people, not scores or marks against our name or a set of scales. Reconciliation with God in the present, even if impossible with his political enemies, will ease Billy's fears of meeting God in a few months' time. The pastor here is not dispenser of divine forgiveness but fellow penitent, helping the individual to tell their story honestly, remorse and all, and ask for forgiveness. In Anglican theology, the priest furthermore declares absolution. To hear from another person that God has forgiven us can provide powerful release from guilt and fear.

Billy's Last Chapter

In Billy's final weeks, he is moved to a hospice. The chaplain detects a subtle attitudinal shift.

A nurse knocks and brings him his medication. He can tell by her name, Mairead, that she is Catholic. Most of his life, he was loath to pronounce what he considered 'foreign names,' but he resolves to acknowledge her today: 'Mairead, is it?' They talk about her children, how they have studied at university but cannot find a job locally, and how it is little wonder young people move away from Northern Ireland 'to get away from this mad place.' Billy senses something of their shared humanity and experience.

On the chaplain's final visit before Billy dies, she turns in her prayer book to the service called Preparation for Death. At the confession, Billy relates for the first time to another person something he did decades ago. Until recently, he was able to justify it, rationalizing that they were different times, or that the end justified the means. He had maintained an unyielding attitude to the situation in Northern Ireland all these years, in part to suppress feelings of guilt. This is why he was afraid to meet a vengeful God in death.

In the end, Billy shifts a fraction in his self-righteous, hostile stance towards people unlike himself. The chaplain thinks, if God can change this inveterate man at the eleventh hour, then there is hope for us all. She takes him by the hand and pronounces the absolution: 'God Almighty, who forgives all who truly repent, have mercy on you, forgive your sins, and keep you in eternal life.' Billy breathes a little more easily in his dying hours.

Mairead attends the funeral and tells others what a 'lovely wee man' Billy was.

Conclusion

As much as we might be enjoying a page-turner, the best of narratives has to end. When I finish a novel, I pause before I put it away. I hold it and ponder its meaning, its humanity, the complexity of the parts as they relate to the whole. There is the sense of an ending. Our lives too are finite, and God will be very interested to hear our version of why we did what we did with the life he gave us.

In C S Lewis' *The Lion, the Witch and the Wardrobe,* Susan realizes that this Aslan who is to return to Narnia is not a man but a lion.[13] She asks Mr and Mrs Beaver if he is safe. They express it perfectly: 'Who said anything about safe? 'Course he isn't safe. But he's good. He's the King, I tell you.' The good news is that our judge is the same Jesus Christ who provides all we need for our lives' redemption, salvation and transformation. He will indeed come again to judge the living and the dead. Denise, Martin, Ray and Billy can each say in their own way, 'Maranatha, come quickly, Lord!'

Notes

1 J Coots and H Gillespie, 'Santa Claus is Comin' to Town,' 1933. Copyright EMI.

2 Liturgical references from the Church of Ireland's *Book of Common Prayer* (Dublin: Columba Press, 2004).

3 C Larkin, *Dispensational Truth* (New York: Cosimo, 2010).

4 B Brown, 'Listening to Shame,' TED Talk, 2012.

5 J Moltmann, *The Coming of God* (London: SCM Press) p 235.

6 www.victimsupport.org.uk

7 W Brueggemann, *Spirituality of the Psalms* (Philadelphia, PA: Paternoster, 2008).

8 B Hume, *To Be a Pilgrim* (London: SPCK, 2009) p 228.

9 P Ricoeur, 'Life in Quest of Narrative,' in D Wood (ed), *On Paul Ricoeur: Narrative and Interpretation* (London: Routledge, 1991).

10 N T Wright, *Jesus and the Victory of God* (London: SPCK, 1996).

11 J K Rowling, *Harry Potter and the Deathly Hallows* (London: Bloomsbury, 2014).

12 Hume, *op cit.*

13 C S Lewis, *The Lion, the Witch and the Wardrobe* (London: Geoffrey Bles, 1950) p 75.